A Good Title is Hard to Find

RICHARD HUNT

RICHARD HUNT

DEDICATION

For Chris, who showed me how to live 'The Life of Riley'.

RICHARD HUNT

CONTENTS

A GOOD TITLE IS HARD TO FIND

PREFACE

This book is for everyone who enjoys poetry - and for those who don't yet know it!

You may have chosen to read this book as you are already a lover of poetry. You may already understand stanzas, be alert and aligned to alliteration, not be stressed by syllables, and take to metaphors and similes like, well...a duck to water. To you the fine diner, nourished by a devouring appetite for language, I say a warm, "thank you", and I hope that you enjoy this eclectic collection of poems.

But I would like to think that we have you, the reader who is reluctant to pick up a poetry book, who may perceive poetry as somehow being out-of-reach or perhaps stuffy, dull, and highbrow - and all those other clichés.

Once upon time I would have certainly pitched my tent in that camp and would have resided in that postcode.

I now believe that poetry can be enjoyed by everyone. Like all the art forms you just need to find the right 'artist' for *you*, whether that be: musicians, painters, actors, comedians, authors…or poets.

This collection of innovative poems aims to illuminate the ordinary and the relatable; some are playful and light-hearted, whilst others focus on the deeper feelings of love, life and loss. Covering observations from: puddings to changing the bed; teabag efficiency to memorable Sundays, and spoon playing to fixing a leaky sink, within these pages there is a connection for everyone.

I hope you enjoy reading them as much as I did writing them.

Oh, and the title…well it is hard to find the right one!

A Good Title is Hard to Find.

Even mixing the word order,
To find a good title is hard,
The Anthem of the Doomed Poet,
Stop all the Clocks,
Whilst I take the time to stand and stare,
Sat on a Fern Hill,
Not Waving but Drowning in a lack of thoughts,
Shall I compare myself to a summer's day?
My thoughts more lonely and more desolate!
The Tyger, The Raven,
Or the Owl and the Pussy Cat might have better ideas?
Do Not Stand at my Poem and Weep,
Bent double and drunk with fatigue,
A sweet and fitting title will arrive soon enough…

A GOOD TITLE IS HARD TO FIND

LOVE

Missing you is...

Missing you is an empty cup and a lonely seat.
Missing you is the Tower without the Pinnacle watching over.

Missing you is...

Missing you is the mill without the stretch of the sky-breaking
chimney.
Missing you is like the lonely, midnight graveyard owl, searching for
prey.

Missing you is...

Missing you is the park's drained boating lake: sunken and adrift.
Missing you is like a Valley with no Parade.

Missing you is...

Missing you is the beck, spilling and spinning without direction.
Missing you is forlorn hung shirts; like dogs pining in wardrobed
kennels.

Missing you is...

Missing you is fish without the chips, a half-empty plate: knotted
stomach and strangled appetite.
Missing you is searching for stars with the lens obscured and a
mournful mocking moon.

Missing you is...

Colleen

A cradle of love.
A smile to lift.
A hug to hide within.
A hand to hold.
Arms to embrace.
Eyes to comfort.
Feet stood firm.
Shoulders to carry the load.
Strength beyond strength.
Kindness to share.
A heart to give and to give again...
Forever an anchor and haven.

If Love Was A Duvet

Fresh and tender, with a gentle touch,
It would gather and comfort and hug so much.
The rain and the scratch of the night on the pane,
Pull it in tight 'til morning again.

If you were ill, sad or unable to move,
This blanket of love would protect and soothe.
And when we get old and threadbare and worn,
This duvet would lay and still keep us warm.

Its stitching would hold, and its love run on,
To calm and give rest when around might be none.
At the end of the day; our forever sleep,
When our eyes are closed for the Earth to keep.

Our duvet will live and last forever,
Silent and soft with the grace of its feather.

If love was a duvet.

Flowers and Wings

She's surrounded, but lonely,
And dreaming if only,
That she could be somewhere else.
The hand she was given,
Was taken, now stricken,
Now searching to find her true self.

The music she listens,
Of dancing and ribbons,
Of laughter, a life lived carefree.
But in bed in fear,
A stranger, her tear,
Another sad trapped memory.

She takes to her garden,
He's stifling and hardened,
A moment of tranquility and peace,
This beautiful girl,
As the petals unfurl,
She's longing for love and release.

When driving she's thinking,
He's sober not drinking,
Now home and she's turning the key.
Bitterness, rage,
No more words on this page,
A chapter she didn't foresee.

Ohhh, and how sweet she sings,
Scented flowers and wings,
To fly and be free.
Ohhh, and the wishes she makes,
And a new life it takes,
To be together, happy.

Courage and strength,
From a life at arm's length,
Determined she walks, but she weeps.
Her wings can take flight,
She's now weightless and light,
Her dreams are not just when she sleeps.

A cottage, a kitten,
Passion and smitten,
Protection from winter and rain.
A blanket, a duvet,
And a love they both knew they,
Would take away sorrow and pain.

Rose-robed and simple,
A place to rekindle,
Safe, serene, soothing and dear.
An embrace, tight and giving,
A tender life-living,
Hearts in rhythm to hear.

A delicate dahlia,
Light, space and saviour,
Nourished and natured to last.
Blossom and colour,
Rich, vibrant and fuller,
A future beginning to cast.

Ohhh, and how sweet she still sings,
Scented flowers and wings,
She has flown and is free.
Ohhh, and the wishes she made,
She's no longer afraid,
At last, together, happy.

Agony Ant

Dear ant,
My love trail is scant,
Please can you help me?

Dear love pigeon,
May I have a smidgeon,
To know what love can be?

Dear cooing birds,
Would it be absurd,
To help me to fly-free?

Dear butterfly,
Can you explain why,
They float inside readily?

Dear entwined swans,
Please respond,
Listen to my plea.

Dear courting rabbits,
With amorous habits,
Help me find a devotee.

Dear caring seahorses,
With romantic forces,
Can you make me happy?

I Love Your Puddings

I'd stumble for your crumble,
I'm keen as custard,
Your sticky toffee pudding,
Gets me hot and flustered!

Blow your flaky pastry,
Your flimsy fondant icing,
It's your gorgeous fruity fillings,
That gets me up and dancing!

I'd lunge for your sponge,
And canoodle for a strudel,
Give me all that stodge,
The whole kit 'n' caboodle!

Your steamy desserts,
Parkin, suet, treacle tart,
Jam in hot rice pudding,
These things capture my heart!

Ice cream melts too quicky,
And sorbets just lack flavour,
It's you I love and all you serve,
To taste, devour and savor.

Reading in the Sun

A smile across your sunlit face,
Your shimmering skin, your happy place.
Deep blue eyes follow the page,
In the warmth I freeze and simply gaze
At you, laying in the heat,
Gentle hands and delicate feet.
I wonder what you're thinking there,
Watching the breeze, dance with your hair,
A moment gone, and then another,
I could watch all day and never bother
To look away, content I'd stay,
Thankful to be with you this way.

Shelter

Daggered rain stabs on my cheek,
Frosted ground beneath our feet.
Warm amber lit lamps don't hide the cold
I'll gather you close to shield and hold.
Burrow your head under my wing,
Wrapped away from the winter sting.
Protect and fend, I'll take the blows,
Keep you warm as our love glows.
The piercing shriek of slicing wind,
Desolate moon, icy-silver ringed.
Frozen earth as hard as stone,
I'll hold you tight to take you home.
Harboured hug to keep you safe,
Tightly held in a snug embrace.
Lips softened, eyes wide, fixed in bliss,
Inside we warm, melt into a kiss.
Then I'll hold you until sleep,
Within my arms secure I'll keep,
I hear you breathe; peaceful, content,
Just like the tender dreams I've dreamt.

The Garden

Winter

Barren birch bracken, bends beneath the burden of its blanketed branches,
Straining towards the hardened cold-hearted earth.
The silhouettes of bronchiole trees wheeze for breath, frozen air too cold to inhale.
The weakened eye of day slides below sheets of cold iron and pale silver.
Sharp shadows clamp to the ridged frost-peaked soil, stretching away, reaching desperately to escape.
Life existing through slumber.
Silent. Still. Waiting to be awoken.

Spring

Peering timidly; shyly beyond the stone-cold grip.
Beauty unveils itself, yet fragile and vulnerable.
Confetti of pink, flirt in the breeze; light carefree and wishful.
A delicate dance by daylight.
But beware the midnight frost, its splintered ice-laced tendrils stealing.
The weaker succumbed and seduced; perished by sunrise.
Heed hail, be weary of wind; on a fine web, nature is balanced.
A promise of hope.

Summer

Comes to captivate and fascinate; revel and reveal; glow and show,
To the soft tune of petunias, sweet dahlias lead the parade.
A buzz of intense colour; a thrum and hum of vivid passion!
The lavender scented breeze strokes the heads of bowing fuchsias as they rest.
Limbs stretch and then pause in the drowsing heat.
Later, fairies fall and glide in the flux of the evening hush.
Amorous, alert and awoken again.

Autumn

Blushing trees surrender to the flirtatious chase of the wistful breeze.
Whisked and frisked, low and high, below and above,
Playful capture and release in the scarlet sun.
By night, frosted together under the devoted gaze of a fingerprint moon.
Clocks rest and rewind to better times ahead.
Satin shackle threads hang from privet, a night's work applauded by dew,
A time to rest and gather, reap, and yield from what was seeded.
Inside a warm glow burns, rekindled and at peace.

It's the Little Things

It's the little things I remember,
Like our walks in the snow in December…

What you said when we met, keeping me dry in the wet,
It's the way that you slept, the notes that I kept,
Holding your hand, as we strolled on the sand,
I think of memories we made, the places we stayed,
The way that you sighed, wiping tears from my eyes,
Trips to the sea, buttered toast with hot tea,
The size of your shoe, the warm presence of you,
The look on your face, the tightest embrace,
Fires that you lit, the clothes that didn't fit,
The way that you sat, your favourite hat,
My hair you'd help comb, and knowing you're home,
Sharing your worries and cares, hearing you coming upstairs,
Silent thoughts in your seat, the puzzles you'd complete,
Watching you dress, birthdays gifts, you making me guess,
Drenched in the rain, the way you'd heal my pain,
It's the songs that you sang, and the nights that you rang,
The words that you wrote, your big winter coat,
My forever support, the midnight buses we caught,
Sunday watching repeats, even the shopping receipts,
The kisses goodnight, you holding me tight,
Our garden in June, the smell of perfume,
The jokes that you told, sheltering me from the cold,
Christmas cards that we'd post, benches on coasts,
Showing stars up above, and the warmth of your love…

Like our walks in the snow in December,
It's the little things I'll remember.

A GOOD TITLE IS HARD TO FIND

SCHOOL

The Greatest Show and Tell

The audience waits, final shoelaces tied,
As the injured and wet return inside.
Hair plaited, noses blown and the classroom hushed,
Cross-legged, arms-folded, toilets flushed.
The day's performance soon ending, the exciting hurrah!
Items kooky, odd and bizarre!
There's been snakeskins, postcards, rocks and bus tickets,
And bullets and eggs have appeared from fluffed pockets.

Today there's a bag, inside a mystery.
Intense, revealed, carefully…
The class is silent, just a punctuated tick
Then from the bag…James pulls a stick…
"So, tell me James why have you brought this?"
"I found it on the way to school Miss."
"Well James, it's splendid, such history,
A stick from a branch of an ancient tree!"

"I've got a tree!" said a shuffle at the back.
"I climb them!" shouted some knees covered in black!
"I love trees!" cooed the ponytail in the middle.
"I haven't got one," wept sad fingers, hair in a twiddle.
"You can share my tree," whispered a kind voice in glasses.
James' stick had certainly inspired the masses!
"…Yes, I know Martha, you have a cat,
But it really is not the time for that!"

Curiosities and treasures on such a scale,
P.T Barnum's worried his circus will fail!
They'll hurry and queue all in line to see
The enchanting delights on display in class 3!
Searching and scrambling for items to tell,
A cactus, a grape and a seaside shell.
"Gasps!" and, "Oohs!" and, "Isn't that swell!'
It's all a show, at Show and Tell!

What Are You Doing After School?

After school, we feel happy and free!
After school, I'm swimming with my sister.
After school, I'm excited, a sleep-over.
After school, I'm riding my bike with friends.
After school, I'm finding sticks to build a tent.
After school, I'm going out for tea.
After school, we're sharing homework.
After school, we're going on holiday.
After school, I'm getting a kitten.
After school, I'm paying my mate a visit.

After school, a life I didn't foresee.
After school, I'm sinking, I've missed her.
After school, I'm tired, a sleep-under.
After school, I'm riding alone, dead ends.
After school, I'm finding money for rent.
After school, I'm feeling hungry.
After school, I'm alone out of work.
After school, I'm going nowhere.
After school, I'm getting frustrated.
After school, I'm paying the bills.

After school, we feel happy and free!
After school, a life I didn't foresee.

Noticed

You said: "Thank you." You noticed me!
Brief, but tummy-flipping.
You saw me. Finally.

We're 3 places apart on the register, sat 2 rows behind.
We also have 5 letters matching in our names.
You have 307 followers - and me.

Remember, I was the first to lend you a pen when you'd forgotten yours?
A pen we have both now held: a connection.
You like pasta on a Monday, with a cheese sprinkle.

You've changed seats again in Chemistry.
I always walk the long way around to my class, just to see your bag.
On Tuesday I saw you laughing at break – that made me happy.

You have PE on Wednesdays, but you missed last week's lesson.
Dentist?
Netball on Thursdays after school.
The number 60 was late again, but you waited in the rain.

And then it happened, on Friday.
I saw you approaching. Heart pounding.
I opened the door. I let you through. And you thanked me!

You noticed me!
Do you like me?

No Ball at Breaktime

When the boy who brings the ball is ill,
Breaktime is punctured and still,
We stare at our shoes,
Kick stones as we choose,
We might start a fight,
Take a hat out of spite,
When the boy who brings the ball is ill.

When the girl who brings the ball is ill,
Breaktime is inflated, a thrill,
We perform in twos,
Talk with whoever we choose,
We might start to write,
Take a hand, check they're alright,
When the girl who brings the ball is ill.

We hope they're both back tomorrow!

World Teachers' Day

Teachers are…

Actors and motivational presenters,
Planners and creative inventors,
Greeters and open day welcomers,
Patient and nurturing developers,
Carers and social workers,
Registrars and forever list makers,
Cobblers and specs fixing opticians,
Problem-solvers making decisions,
Discipliners and sympathizers,
Surveyors of playtime reconcilers,
Disco-dancers and enthusiastic singers,
Bringers and servers of dinners,
Advisers and analysts of data,
Applauding prize-giving celebrator,
Financers and trip debt collectors,
Scriptwriters and play choreographers,
Nose-wipers and gravel grazed knee healers,
The help-you-ride-on-a-bike-two-wheelers,
Itinerary makers and visit risk assessors,
The putting-hair-in-a-ponytail-before-PE hairdressers,
Librarians and information technology specialists,
The blue-paper-towel-nurses and the tooth-in-a-tissue-dentists,
Communicators and spokesmen and spokeswomen,
Coaches and instructors of swimming,
Emergency first responders and health experts,
Breakfast givers, and lifters of lids from yoghurts,
Artistic directors and stage backdrop painters,
Photocopiers and end of day cleaners.

And…they also teach.

Test Instructions versus Life Instructions

Test instruction	Life instruction
Don't talk.	Talk and listen kindly.
Don't copy.	Share.
This is a timed test. Work through the test until you are asked to stop.	Be more than a measure of time and age.
Don't write outside the answer box.	Explore, experience and exist.
Don't crumple your answer booklet.	You will get crumpled, but laughter lines make the deepest creases. Be someone's reason to smile. Make someone laugh today.
Pay particular attention to any instructions.	Listen and learn from those you respect.
You should try to answer all the questions.	Some answers you'll never find nor understand: move on.
Put your hand up and wait for someone to come to you.	Be independent, be proactive, don't wait for things to happen.
Rub out the answer you don't want the marker to see.	You will make mistakes that can't be erased, each one an opportunity to be a better person; learn from them. Be your own marker.
Work as quickly as you can.	Be patient, rest when you need to.
There are different types of question.	There are different types of people: you can learn from them all, be tolerant.
Use only blue or black ink.	Colour your life with a vibrant palette.
I'll tell you when there are five minutes left.	Life can be painfully short; you don't know when it will end, embrace each minute.
Put your pencil down, the test is over.	No one will remember your test score. But they'll remember how you made them feel. Do good things before the test is over.

Teacher types in haiku

The Decliner

It's getting much worse,
Education hasn't learnt,
It will get worse still.

The Resigner

I'm leaving again,
I know I've said it before,
Supermarket shelves.

The Whiner

I moan at you lots,
About everything daily,
A blackhole of doom.

The Dodger

I'm not here again.
Hide and seek school champion,
Finding my sicknote.

The Revolver

Spin! Give me a swerve!
Everything comes full circle,
I am still sat here.

The Pollinator

Drone on a mission,
Spreading my woes, I'll sting you,
Bitter for pity.

The Spiritualiser

Beads, sandals, crystals,
Just the right side of hippy,
Calming lavender.

The Inappropriator

No filter in place,
Your jokes can be a disgrace,
Foot-in-mouth misplace.

The Enforcer

String them up, thrash, maim!
Slipper, lines, detention, cane!
Disciplines the game.

Newby

Excited, wide-eyed,
Eager, ambition, enthused,
Not yet cynical.

The Feeder

Seeking snacks and treats,
Staffroom to cupboard to fridge,
Hungry for learning.

The Collector

Hands-up, where's the cash?
Tea fund, milk money, sweepstake,
Empty your pockets!

The Recliner

Begins upright calm,
Then lounges, slow rock, now benched,
Bottom set maths next.

RICHARD HUNT

LIFE AND LOSS

"You have one missed call."

Sorry I missed your call.
Was I doing anything special?
The bins could have overflowed,
The dishwasher could have been left unemptied,
I should have had the TV on mute,
I should have had the radio turned down,
The doorbell could have waited,
The hot water could have gone cold,
I should have left the bed unmade,
I should have left the furniture thick with dust,
The car could have been unwashed,
The grass could have been left overgrown,
Sorry I missed your call.

Sorry I missed your call.
I wonder still, could I have saved you?
Rescued you, freed you?
Could I have changed anything?
What would I have said?
Could I have stopped the falling?
Reached in and pulled you out?
Sorry I missed your call.

Sorry I missed your call.
Do I feel guilty or blessed?
It may have been a secretary, a delivery, a friend,
There is no comfort in an appointment reminder.
Now forever at the end of the phone,
Cherished and protected, your voice in safe keeping.
I listen to you - and that one missed call each day,
You told me you loved me.
I missed you and now you're yearned forever,
You'll always be *The One* – missed call.

Read to Me

Kneeling by your bed I'd read:

We read of adventures and heroes and gallant knights,
Of ships and exploring and spacemen on flights.

We'd read them once, you'd listen, folded in tight,
We'd read them again, you'd remember, learnt by site.

When older you'd read on your own, learn value and worth,
You'd read about music, stars and Earth.

Readings at weddings, birthdays and celebrations,
Readings of love to mark special occasions.

And I now kneel by your flowerbed and read:

I read of a life full of exploring and bright,
Of your adventures, our hero, our gallant knight.

Absent Calendar

Tear down the stockings and pull them to thread,
Chop up the tree, chastised to the shed.
Silence the Carols, put the tv on mute,
Lock the door, no visitors, no red suit.

Rip up the cards and melt down the snow,
Stop the bells chiming, let the tears flow.
Block out the lights, no mistletoe kiss,
Freeze celebrations, return gifts.

The countdown has ended, the sadness begun,
The star has faded, the loss of our son.
This Christmas, the next, and the next, and forever
Remembered always, until we're together.

I Wonder?

I wonder....
Did you have a happy life?
Do you have regrets?
Did you achieve all you wanted?
What plans had you made?
What did you still wish to accomplish?
Did you leave satisfied?
What friendships or enemies did you have?
Did you die alone?
Who did you leave behind?
Have you found what you were searching for?
Have you met a loved one who passed before?
Had you had enough?
What advice would you give?
What do you miss?
Have you made friends?
Are you afraid?
Do the seasons feel the same?
Would you have changed anything?
Do you still have worries?
Was it worth worrying?
Do you laugh?
Do you feel pain?
Were you content?
Did you find love?
Were you loved?
Can you hear me?
Are you lonely?
Do you have visitors?
Do you get cold at night?
What would you say about the news?
Are you resting in peace?
Do you know you're missed?
I wonder all these things still.

Lifeline*

Make your line significant.
Make it magnificent.
Make it wide, fill it with experiences.
Travel along your line without fear, let it veer, visit and voyage.
Meet people, talk to people, listen to people.
Be helpful, but don't be afraid to be helped.
Be generous with your time, but take your time, and value time.
Be busy, be still. Switch on – switch off.
Be remembered and lovingly remember others.
Love, and let others love you.
Feel proud, be loud, make a stand – raise your point.
Look after others, the vulnerable, let others take care of you.
Play music, learn a language, run.
Run fast – be a leader, run slow – let others past, be a supporter.
Make someone laugh, but don't be too proud to be laughed at.
Feel the sun, watch the clouds and touch the cold, weather all.
Share and borrow, lend and take.
Rub your line out, start again, change direction.
Make your line unique, make it unparalleled, make it steep.
Make it twist, turn, take-off and land.
Make it direct, or let it wander.
Make it what you want – draw your line, live your life.

> *Lifeline: the dash between your dates (born – died).
> For my hero Walter.*

Where the Crocuses Grow

The home bell rings,
No school tomorrow,
And the children laid their flowers where the crocuses grow.

Messages written,
Giving words to sorrow,
And the children laid their flowers where the crocuses grow.

Silent mourners,
Behind the coffin follow,
And the children laid their flowers where the crocuses grow.

The cows bowed their heads,
As the fields lay in fallow,
And the children laid their flowers where the crocuses grow.

Dirt and flowers cast,
As the tears began to flow,
And the children laid their flowers where the crocuses grow.

Dedicated to George Lewis, September 2021

RICHARD HUNT

HEALTH AND WELL-BEING

Back Pain

Severed sleep,
Lacerations slash the peace,
Tearing and scraping,
Clawing and scratching at nerves.
The jagged knife withdraws,
Then fiercely spears more deeply,
Slicing and scouring beneath flesh.

Wait. A truce? Quiet.
Pausing, waiting, still….
Aaarrrrrrrrr! Off-guard, a serrated dagger pierces!

A shock, intense and sharp, jolts the tension,
A surged cutting incision.
Tormented and tortured within.
Please stop.

Closed for Maintenance

Down for emergency maintenance,
Apologies for any inconvenience.
There has been a disruption to the service planned,
Just cleaning things up, it's all in hand.
404 error, file path and page not found,
Offline, off-grid, gone underground.
Updating security and making bug fixes,
Been experiencing technical difficulties.
Need to reboot, unplug and start again,
Login later to access this domain.
Networking notworking, under construction,
A temporary loss, a brief obstruction.
Required repairs, too much data,
Please try again or come back later.
Scheduled downtime, will shortly be back,
Adding new features, back on track.

Chair of Despair

I arrive positive and helpful and take a seat.
Hot tea, biscuits and fondness.

Are you sitting comfortably? Then we'll begin...

A small weight is added,
It starts with a slight shifting.
An attempt to remain upbeat on upholstery,
Uncomfortable but a resilient posture remains.

A burden is added, then a suffering tale.
Unnoticeable at first,
But a creak and a sigh are released.

Another weight, then another,
Heavier and heavier.

Support wains and energy seeps,
I'm starting to sink slowly,
Gasping for breath.
Then guilt is added, a cumbersome mass,
Followed by pressure and worry,
The strain is now visible.

A demand and several woes are placed like blocks.
Falling further and further.
More sorrow is poured,
Now I'm a decliner in the recliner.

Pulled, plunged and plummeting
Towards the floor...then...

"More tea? Another biscuit?"
No thanks. I'm full.
I can't take anymore.

Hide and Seek

Count to ten, hide, on the run,
Undercover, disguised, the game has begun…
Important, promotion, top of the tree.
Lonely, demoted, we were too blind to see…
New car, new shirt, hasn't he done well?
Punctured, unbuttoned, no one could tell…
Swilling pints, telling jokes, star of the show!
Though, glass half empty, drunk with sorrow…
Smiles and nods like heading balloons.
Whilst trudging, boots leaden, on wet afternoons…
Popular, cheerful, one of the lads!
Half-mast, frayed, hoist the red flags…
Well hidden, in shadows, don't be afraid to speak,
To the recluse champion of hide and seek.

A poem for World Suicide Prevention Day.
In Remembrance of Jack Barraclough.

I - solated.

Periphery, perimeter and postponed.
Inessential, inordinate and insignificant.
Outside, outskirts and outlier.
Unnecessary, unrequired and unneeded.
Superfluous, surplus and substitute.
Sparse, spare and spurned.
Rejected, residue and redundant.
Excluded, extinguished and external.
Alienated, alone and almost.
Debris, desolate and destitute…

Isolated

WEATHER AND SEASONS

Heatwave

Heat waved,
A worn goodbye,
Scorched gardens left behind,
Rivers taken and summer too,
Stormed out.

Recent Rainfall

Raindrops regimentally rally on wire,
Reluctantly they relinquish restraint: rain...drops.
A reticent rainbow fades, rapidly returning to rest.
Rain reliant roses recover and reveal.
Rhododendrons relish, rejoice and reprise.
Recent rainfall replenishes.

Suffocated Awake

Suffocated awake,
End this arid misery,
Hallucinations of solace and peace.
Enslaved by night's chains, they stretch and turn me this way then
that and back again.
Endless gasping at stale dry air into coarse parched sacks,
Imprisoned and crushed by its intensity.
Each endless moment spent with grazed swallowing over a
scratched throat.
Morning brings light and a drought of energy,
A brief respite until night returns.

Sutton Beck

Along Sutton Beck,
Nettles lean into the path, sniffing out ankles.
Leaves tiring, choosing who will fall first.
Grates choke on a palette of deciduous waste,
As a stick panics, before going under.
Roses wave goodbye to summer,
Whilst unfinished garden projects are grounded.
Distant drilling competes with drifting radio muffles,
Seductive blackberries entice to be picked; fingers licked and pricked.
A woollen hat hangs waiting on bracken for its head to return,
Artificial grass can't hide Autumn's confetti,
Above, crows survey fields and call of their findings.
September, along Sutton Beck.

RICHARD HUNT

MISCELLANEOUS

Recipe for Disaster (A Meal for Two)

Resentfully pour a pint of spilt milk,
Drain in a dose of soured cream,
Dredge with a splintered wooden spoon,
Slouch on a tepid heat, leaving to simmer and brood.
Meanwhile, melt aspirations in a large pan of failure,
Dump in a knob of crumb-soiled butter,
Whisk in some deep dissatisfaction.
Scorch with roughly grated sarcasm and a sharp pinch of chilli,
Beat in curdled eggs.
Add all ingredients to the melting pot,
Place in a blackened oven for as long as it takes.
Parboil stubborn hearts until softened,
Steep in disappointment until limp,
Season with regret and serve cold.

Sneering suggestion:

A nip of lemon will add some bite (but remove any zest).

Dress:

Wear white (accessorize with a stain of tomato sauce).

Whine:

For a suitable bitter and dry finish, try an acidic and acetic whine with
heady off-notes of remorse.

Bed-Vroom Pitstop (or Changing the Bed)

Bed framed in place.

Alarm clock started.

GO! GO! GO!

Pluck! Pillowcases wrenched and removed.
Dash! Duvet heaved and hauled.
Quick! Quilt dragged and pulled.
Shazam! Sheets on, folded, tucked.
Spring! Suspension checked and coiled.
Pronto! Pyjamas pressed and placed.
Throw! Furnishings plumped and spread.

Alarm clock stopped.

The Grand Prix? To sleep on the winner's podium.

Checkout These Deals!

Gravy stock clearance,
Blinds…closing-down sale,
Unwanted items…discounted,
Cats…retailed here!

Lamb joints chopped,
Curtains curtailed,
Clothes alterations…10% off,
Cut price razors!

Value eggs…won't be beaten,
Cream…double discount,
Dead batteries…free of charge,
Stationery marked down!

Meat costs carved,
Sails…for sale for sailing,
Flowers cut,
Cost of bread…unraised!

Candles reduced,
Faulty TVs too good to turn down,
Orange juice squeezed,
Haircut fees trimmed!

Playing card deals,
Boxing gloves at knock down prices,
Price of onions sliced,
Light bulbs on/off-er.

Fish Butty RIP

Solemnly we lay this fish to bed,
Between two sides of buttered bread.
Our hearts like butter they softly melt,
The crunch of batter, hot vinegar smelt.

And so this fish lay warm and sleeping,
It's resting place in safe keeping.
Held fondly, a final destiny,
Farewell, goodbye, into my tummy.

17 Syllables

Not my fa-vour-ite,
Type of po-em the Hai-ku,
I run out of syll-

Never Buy a Four-Place Toaster

Never buy a four-place toaster,
You don't need space 3 or 4,
You only bought it just to boast to
Friends, that you could toast more.

Here We Go! Here We Go! Here We Go! (Haiku)

The football season,
Hope, ambition and belief,
Here we go! (times 3).

Spider haiku

Spider in the bath,
Eight 'leg-bands', all inflated.
Front crawl to the taps!

Oh no!

And in she came again...
A wasp with an issue.
A moth draining your light.
A fly beating on your ear drums.
A dog harassing your very bones.
A whale, drowning you in drones.
I should be patient,
I should be stronger, but
None ever wished she stayed longer.

The Garden Fete (worse than death)

Severed grass, lays strewn in parts,
Whilst washing lines hang life-less.
Pegs cling desperately to sodden towels,
A tug of war with gravity before plummeting.
Wind fires indiscriminately at shying plant pots,
Smashing to the ground, their petals of red dispersed.
Roses harshly tied torturously to walls,
Now forlorn and barely feeling the sun.
Obliterated leaves scatter the lawn,
Branches torn from parents lay snapped, broken and orphaned.
Insects gasp for breath, drowning in puddles and ponds,
Captured, the fly waits…
How sweet does the garden grow?

Golf!

SWISH!

No birdie, albatross or eagle,
Is swearing on the course illegal?

SLICE!

Driver, putter and swing,
I don't think golf is my thing!

PULLED!

Hazard, bunker and rough,
Home! I've had enough!

MISS!

Back nine, fore, 19th hole,
Patience waning, lost control.

SWIPE!

Woods, irons, leather gloves
Do I still have the receipt for these clubs?

WHOOPS!

Divots dug and the most shots played,
Surely the highest score, the Master, a champion made.

HOORAY!

I must've been wrong, a great technique!
I'll be back again same time next week!

Like a Sink Over Troubled Water

I'm feeling weary,
Not slept at all,
Tears are in my eyes,
Under the sink I crawl.
I'm on my side,
Oh, I've had enough,
And I'm on the ground.
Like a sink over troubled water,
The leak will be found!
Like a sink over troubled water,
I will not be drowned!
When I'm down and out,
When I'm off my feet,
When evening falls, searching hard,
I will find you,
I'll take you apart,
Oh, when the water runs,
And soaking all around.
Like a sink over troubled water,
The leak will be found!
Like a sink over troubled water,
I will not be drowned!

Madame Waggett's* Patisserie

*pronounced *wa – jays*

We invite you to visit the finest patisserie in the whole of 'Paree'!
Come one and all to…Madame Waggett's patisserie!

If croissants and fondants are what you fancy,
Room for macaroons, take your chance, eh?
The finest baker in the whole of France, yeh!
Affectionately, fanatically, especially made for you and me!
At Madame Waggett's patisserie!

You'll be in a whirl for her profiterole!
Her eclairs are devoured and eaten whole!
She's the greatest chef with the sweetest soul!
Eagerly, delightfully, confectionary for you to see!
At Madame Waggett's patisserie!

Cakes, chocolate gateaux and buns!
Tartes and turnovers for your tums!
It's the place where everybody runs!
Emphatically, splendidly, a sensational bakery
At Madame Waggett's patisserie!

Choux a la crème, so tempting and nice!
Custards, bakes, vanilla slice!
So good you'll want to order twice!
Fantasy, delicacy, amazing cakes we all agree!
At Madame Waggett's patisserie!
At Madame Waggett's patisserie!

None of Your Business?

Disinterest rates rising,
You'll be fine not surprising!

Wheat production cropped,
Exports blocked.

Generators won't be generated,
Contracts to be terminated.

String, wool and cotton lines cut,
Shops to be shut.

Window and door production to be closed,
Housebuilding bulldozed.

Yard sticks not made any longer,
Extra strong mints not made stronger.

Curtains and blinds' trade to shut down,
Estates agents moved out of town.

Key turners bolted and locked,
Shipbuilding docked.

Paper factory to fold,
Ice cream sellers left out in the cold.

Lift supplies have stopped going up,
Industry set to breakup.

Car manufacturing driven out,
Bath purchases have hit a drought.

Tiling and carpets have been floored,
Pubs closed; last orders poured.

None of your business?

Rat Inside my Poem!

Drat! There's a *rat* inside my poem!
It's there sc*rat*ching and i*rat*e!
Its hiding is first *rat*e!
As though it has evapo*rat*ed or emig*rat*ed!
I'm *rat*her *rat*tled and be*rat*ed.
My inner w*rat*h is *rat*ified!
I seek to libe*rat*e this *rat* inside.
Please can we collabo*rat*e?
Or mode*rat*ely, coope*rat*e?
There maybe more, an unfair *rat*io,
Oh *rat*, you simply have to go!
G*rat*ifying, exhila*rat*ing,
Start the celeb*rat*ing!
The *rat* is finally on the run,
Cong*rat*s!
No! Now there's more than one!

Where has my Mouse Gone?

Eek! Where's it gone?
Under my footer, above my header, in the cloud?
Deserted under the desktop?
A floorboard beneath the keyboard?
The recycling bin, amongst shredded documents?
Timid amidst this text? Flaunting behind fonts?
Watching under a watermark? Obscured under a table?
Statuesque, hidden by a column? Buried betwixt page breaks?
Stashed below the cache? Screened beneath the screen?
Peering through windows?
Strolled whilst I scrolled? How can it be so bold?
Search, find, scan…
Oh, there it is. Little scallywag!
Like a white arrow zooming across my screen.
Lured by clickbait.

Spoons (for Jonny)

It was the talent show,
On a knife edge, the audience waited,
His dream, his goal, ambition, intent,
It was all he had anticipated.

Jonny took out his souped-up spoons,
He'd buffed them quite brightly,
The audience stirred in anticipation,
With a grin he started lightly.

Clack, clack, clickety-clack,
He soon picked up the pace,
And as the crowd began to clap
A smile came across his face!

He played his spoons with passion,
His tongue out on display,
Concentrating on his rhythm,
The crowd began to sway!

"This is such a talent," a young boy said,
"Who is this clever man?"
"It's Jonny and his spoons," I shouted!
As raucous chants began!

The throng soon started dancing,
As his spoons whisked up a beat,
Whirling, twirling, leaping,
They moved their happy feet!

His spoons made people happy,
Some even began to cry,
He'd won the competition,
They lofted him up high!

Jonny had a talent,
He felt free and liberated.
For spoons are not just for stirring,
They can be celebrated!

The Stationery War

The rulers ruled and declared civil war,
The cabinet wasn't big enough anymore.
They measured a plan, the felt tips advising,
The rulers underlined this strategy for resizing.
The stationery marched to the rubber band,
Staples clasped to their arms in hand.

Pencils were drawn and began to lead,
Hole punchers punched at lightning speed.
In a scissor formation, the paper folded in fright,
Whilst the pens attacked from the right.
Sharpeners grinded and spun into action,
Compasses covered angles in every direction.

The stencils cut through, guiding others along,
Ink cartridges were toned, resolute and strong.
Files filed past amongst the doom,
The gel pens stuck together and formed a platoon.
Shavings lay strewn and ink had bled,
Papers were shredded and envelopes had fled.

Seeing the carnage, a truce was called,
The rulers wished for peace reinstalled.
The stationery set down their weapons,
The Last Post-it was played amongst blunted crayons.
The war halted, stationary, and to no avail,
Please take stock of this stationery tale.

Teabag Efficiency

Dear humble teabag, I want to thank you,
For your steadily patient bathing stew,
For these are the things you've allowed me to do…

Fill the dishwasher, empty the bin,
Pour cereal, scratch an itch on my skin.
Plump cushions, polish shoes,
Read emails, tut at the news.
Take out the meat to defrost,
Hang out clothes, put more in to wash.
Smell the milk, take out a spoon,
Search for a biscuit, dance like a loon.
Feed the fish, stroke the cat,
Look out and ponder about this and that.
Tighten my belt, put on socks,
Talk to the dog, whilst doing squats.
Wonder about bin day. Tune in the radio,
Fold a tea towel, watch the breakfast show.
Check the weather, button up my coat,
Update social media, find the remote.
Butter some toast, pick up crumbs,
Help to do homework sums.
Change the battery on a clock,
Worry about traffic gridlock.
Change a lightbulb, send a text,
Remember holidays, where to next?
Look outside, hillsides for viewing,
Fall in a trance, forget it was brewing!

The next time you're waiting for a cup of tea,
Remember teabag efficiency!

ON / OFF

Big coat: ON
Woolly gloves: ON
Vehicle headlamps: ON
Curtains pulled: ON
Amber streetlights: ON
TV's 'Strictly': ON
Car demister: ON
Scented candles: ON
Privets with webs: ON
Thick socks: ON
Stewing pot: ON
Cosy slippers: ON
Hot chocolate with marshmallows: ON
Halloween adverts: ON
Christmas countdown: ON!
What's not switched: ON?

Heating: OFF

Trickle Down

Trickle down, drain and let it ooze,
Showered in cold austerity we didn't choose.
Slithering you bathe and quaff your bubbles,
As we sponge and scrub and forget our troubles.

Splash the cash, revel and rollick,
Grateful for the drips as you frolic.
Wash away our lice, scabs and scars,
We praise you for this dribble of ours.

Warm, content, steamy filled to the top,
Indebted, we hold our tongues for a drop.
Cleansed and righteous, full of froth,
We say thank you, with caps to doff!

How grateful we are, purified by the trickle down,
A baptism in putrid bath water as we drown,
Wallow and bask, you've earned it you ought to,
But beware don't empty us out with the bath water…

The Procrastination Club

Stalled of what to do? Join the Procrastination Club!

A warm welcome is guaranteed (when you finally arrive).
We have an extensive drinks menu for you to pour over.
With *mulled-over wine* available at Christmas.
Chew over our excellent menu, perfect for the ponderous palate.
For the puzzling ponderer, our quiz night is held each Thursday.
And there is Music at 7pm every Friday from the resident band, 'Shilly-Shally', so don't dilly-dally! *

*As these events are popular, guests may contemplate arriving sooner…or later.

Uncertain? There's no doubting you'll have a great time!
Don't prolong! We can't wait to see you – in due course.
Dawdle on down to The Procrastination Club!

Directions:

If travelling by train remember to stay on track.
We are a short meander from the station.
Don't diverge or ramble off course.
It should take around 5 minutes, so give yourself an hour.

The Procrastination Club: where uncertainty is a certainty.

Safety notice: On entry we kindly ask that patrons don't linger or loiter in the lobby.

For more info don't hesitate to get in touch.

Keyboard holiday

Esc work.

Del the stress.

Insert a break.

Caps to visit.

Ctrl your life.

Alt the pace.

Enter tranquility.

Shift focus.

Space to relax.

Brightness increased.

Function better.

Return to work.

End.

Sunday

The smell of bacon, egged us from our sleep,
We were easy, life simple, uncomplicated and cheap.
Slow breakfasts, love songs and crumbs on sheets,
A black and white film on a black and white telly, watching repeats.
Giant heavy papers, with sections galore,
Turning the pages to find out the score.
Cartoons, leisure, business and reading the sport,
Competitions to post and the scandals they'd report.

Gardens mown, cars polished and cleaned,
Driven to nowhere, automobile-autopilot, or so it seemed.
Lulled into long, lazy, lounging, leisurely and lethargic afternoons,
Then the countdown of the forty most popular tunes.
Chocolate biscuits and tea and family games indoors,
Roast dinners with cabbage steam clinging to windows.
Town centres deserted, hundreds-thousands eating trifle desserts,
Packed lunches jam-packed, and straightened out shirts.

A Sunday service of buses and churches,
Songs of Praise, school bags sorted and uniform searches.
Shoes polished, homework completed and taking baths,
Bunkered-in, curtains closed; Open All Hours for laughs.
London's Burning, Bullseye and watching Bread,
With the Last of the Summer Wine drank, we got poured into bed.
Sunday's nearly gone, that sweet bouquet,
The 24-hour protection and saviour from Monday.

RICHARD HUNT

ABOUT THE AUTHOR

Richard Hunt is a poet and a former primary school headteacher from Shipley, Yorkshire, who now lives in North Yorkshire. After over 20 years working in education, he began following his dream to become a writer. His innovative poems illuminate the ordinary and the relatable; some are playful and light-hearted and show his adoration of language and word play; whilst others focus on the deeper feelings of love, life and loss.

Son of a factory worker and dinner lady, his hobnailed boots are firmly on the ground. He follows Bradford City, loves the Beatles and presents a local radio show: "Poems, Lyrics and Music." He is probably best known for being the Bradford U-10 Chess Champion, 1985…

A GOOD TITLE IS HARD TO FIND

Printed in Great Britain
by Amazon

87865868R00048